I0137597

Domestication

Rob Hardy

Collected Poems 1996-2016

Up On Big Rock Poetry Series
SHIPWRECKT BOOKS PUBLISHING COMPANY
Rushford, Minnesota

IN®
DIE

Cover painting by Lilla Johnson
Design by Shipwreckt Books

Copyright 2017 Shipwreckt Books
Copyright 1996-2016 Rob Hardy
All rights reserved
ISBN 10:0-9968909-3-9
ISBN 13:978-0-9968909-3-9

Contents

To Clara, Will, and Peter,
and to my mother

Preface

I wrote my first poem in fifth grade. It went like this:

Cold and dreary, weak and weary,
I roam the frozen North,
To and fro the wind does blow
as slowly I trudge forth,
Day and night I try to light
A warm and blazing fire—
It goes out, in vain I shout,
And then I start to tire.
It's eighty below and the freezing snow
Is drifting all around me.
Without a sound, I fall to the ground:
Death has finally found me.

I grew up in Central New York, in the Finger Lakes, where
there's a lot of lake effect snow. More snow even than we get in
Minnesota. I walked to school every day, three-quarters of a mile,
which to a child seems like an epic journey. In the winter I
pretended to be an Arctic explorer, struggling through the huge
snow drifts, frost-bitten, lost in a blizzard.

My mother thought I was a child prodigy, and she signed me
up for a writer's workshop at a place in Ithaca called the
Women's Community Building. It was the mid-1970s. At the
workshop there was me, a ten-year old boy, and a roomful of
middle-aged women. I had brought my death in the Arctic poem.
We sat in a big circle and took turns reading our poems, and the
room went quiet as each woman read. There were poems about
motherhood, domesticity, gardening, and sex. There were poems
about all aspects of the feminine experience. Each poem ended in

appreciative silence or a collective sigh. The I recited my poem about freezing to death. The women gave me a standing ovation. I was a poet.

I continued to write poetry in middle school and high school before taking a long detour into academia that ended in a dissertation on the Roman poet Vergil and a Ph.D. in classics. Along the way, I married a fellow classicist who landed a teaching position at Carleton College in Northfield, Minnesota. I was back in the frozen north, for real this time. After the birth of our first son in 1991, I became a stay-at-home father. It was fatherhood and the everyday round of domestic work, along with a strong desire to belong to this place where I found myself, that brought me back to writing poetry. In some ways, I had entered the world of those women who had first recognized me as a poet. Poetry was an act of homemaking.

It was through poetry, much more than through the mere chance of living here, that I became a Minnesotan. Poetry became a map to help me make my way into this new place. Twenty years after I moved here, my poetry literally became a part of the map of Northfield when one of my poems was stamped into concrete in Bridge Square as the first of Northfield's sidewalk poems.

Although I've traveled extensively in the past few years, and even spent a year living in England, most of my poems stick close to home. The real journey in my poems is spiritual. The early poems were written by someone who grew up going to church, and who continued to be an active member of a church in Northfield. The influence can be felt in early poems like "Packing the Creche" and "Cicadas," both of which first appeared in the magazine *The Christian Century*. In *33 Minnesota Poets*, I wrote that "most of my poetry arises from the same source as my perpetually lapsing Christianity." In recent years, that faith has lapsed more permanently, but the influence remains strong, and is still felt in later poems like "Agnostic Psalm" and "*Baptisia Alba*." As I explained in *33 Minnesota Poets*: "For me, prayer is an invitation to distractions, but poetry centers my mind on an experience, an object, an impulse which becomes more numinous in the concentrated effort to sustain and express that original inspiration in words. I feel an instant recognition when Maxine Kumin speaks of poetry as 'an act of worship,' as 'a state of the soul,' as 'the scratching of a divine itch.'"

In the winter of 2013, a serious ski accident left me lying on my back in the snow, unable to move. I was afraid that life was imitating art, and that my fifth-grade poem would prove prophetic. I was eventually found and rushed in an ambulance to Northfield Hospital. As I was taken out of the ambulance, a doctor appeared at my side and asked me my name. When I told him, he asked, "Aren't you the poet?" It was comforting to know that, if I died that day, I had at least achieved a modest local reputation as a poet. But I didn't die. Three years later, I was chosen to serve as Northfield's first Poet Laureate. I've never been a prolific poet, but regularly being called upon to write poems for City Council meetings and community events has dramatically increased my productivity. Only one of those poems ("The Acting Cashier") appears in this collection: the rest belong to the next phase of my life as a poet.

None of this would have been possible without the support of many people along the way. My deepest thanks go to my wife Clara, my sons Will and Peter, my mother Mimi Hardy, and the Hardy, Shaw, and Houlgate families. I am also deeply indebted to the editors who have done the most to support me as a poet: Emilio and Monica DeGrazia and Ginny Lowe Connors (Grayson Books). Thanks also to Tom Driscoll for his persistence and steady hand in making this book possible. Thanks also to all the friends who have supported and inspired me as a writer through the years. It would be impossible to compile an exhaustive list, but such a list would definitely include Kerry Langan, Tom Van Nortwick, Ruth Weiner, Mary Dunnewold, Jeff Ondich, Peytie McCandless, Cecilia Cornejo Sotelo, Jane McWilliams, Bonnie Jean Flom, Leslie Schultz, and Jessica Peterson White (Content Bookstore). Finally, thanks to the Northfield Public Library, the Northfield Arts and Culture Commission, the Northfield Arts Guild, the First United Church of Christ, and the people of Northfield, Minnesota.

Domestication
Poems 1996 – 2001

Naturalization

The women, the settler's wives,
brought with them bottles
of seeds culled from the east,

rootstock wrapped
in dirty muslin, orphaned
and sentimental weeds.

In some places even now
the butter-and-eggs
and the chicory break out

like a virus

where once a homestead
stood on the corner
of a quarter-section claim,

filling the roadside
with a terminal homesickness.

Packing the Crèche

Petals scab and peel, blackened afterbirth,
poinsettia thinning to a knuckled stalk,
winter whitening like a scar. Already
the fevered aisles are flush with hearts.
By the lectionary, the disciples stare snow-blind
at the transfigured Christ, Lazarus dies: but here
the Magi wait, the shepherds tune their pipes,
the angel of the Lord still fidgets on her thread,
the baby Jesus lies cradled in familiar dust.
Before the crèche is transfigured into bric-à-brac,
I swaddle the sheep in tissue two by two,
old hatbox of an ark, kings and cattle stowed,
angel furled, riding the rising flood
of available light. An early thaw tempts the earth
into expectation, birds modulate into spring.
Two shepherds, left high and dry by Lent,
still tune their pipes, still look into the undecorated sky
for the angel, still wonder where they will find
the manger, the child, their own flocks.

Domestication

The starched breezes off Narragansett Bay
smelled mostly of fish,
but on some fog-bound mornings
the air smelled of damp laundry,
as if the fog itself had poured
from dryer exhausts all across the city,
hanging heavy and wet
until it came dry in the sun.
                At blue midday,
heading for the Block Island Ferry,
the naked sea flashed at every turn,
tattooed with sails,
a zipper of broken docks
open at the shore. My roving eye
was in love with the homeless
heartbreak of waves, the sea-restlessness.
I dreamed of ships,
pregnant sails, hulls bellied
with Swedish ancestors,
chests of linen, Bibles, English phrasebook—
Brukar ni vara sjösjuk?
Are you ever seasick?
—and the sea became
a domestic thing,
smell of laundry, Bible leather,
salt of my own flesh.
                Back at home,
downwind from the cereal factory,
I hang my sheets like
bleached sails billowing
over the dry bones of the inland sea.
My roving eye has been
domesticated to the slow heave of the earth,

winter's tide turning,
the hem of broken fields
mended with a stitch of green.
My laundry flaps and dries
in the malted breeze, as if the morning
itself had risen in the steam
from bowls of hot cereal
all across the city.

Falling

for Ruth and Jason
August 23, 1997

You already know about love.
You fall in love. Falling is easy. Maybe you don't
see it coming.
Maybe you brace yourself against the wind in the door,
see the earth circling below
and jump. Falling is easy. It feels like flight.
You feel your kinship with clouds, with light,
stuff of stars, atoms that float and fall,
meteors, stars that still glow
with the start of everything.
You raise your arms like wings. Butterfly
or belly-flop. You feel the earth expanding—
don't look down. Reach for the cord.
Falling is easy. But is this love
or gravity? Pull the cord. Yes—
love blossoms from the weight you carry,
the question, the tug at your heart.
The parachute pops like a cork.
Now you float in the arms of the atmosphere,
milkweed floss, dandelion seed,
no longer afraid to take root in the earth—
but still floating a while, ecstasy and trust, your high-
altitude heart settling back into a steadier beat,
the tilt of the earth, seasons and days.
But here you are floating—buoyed by invitations
and arrangements. Now you look down.
The ground looms like a date, circled for a landing.
The fields look like RSVPs. Your feet touch. The parachute
falls around you like a wedding dress.
You've landed together. Dance while the earth steadies
beneath your feet. Hold each other up.
Now you will walk together into ordinary days.

Your parachute may become a maternity dress, a mortgage,
a tissue for your tears. It may be divided into diapers,
waterproof sheets, a layette, stories to tell your grandchildren.
Days may come when you forget how it felt to float.
But still this moment of landing lives inside you,
when the touch of the ground felt like a vow—
I will always be there. I will catch you if you fall.

Essential Love

Place the palm of your hand
flat against your cheek,
push outward against
the inside
with your tongue—
this is how it feels, only
smoother, tighter,
rounder. And you know
your tongue's a tongue—
but what's this?
An elbow? A knee?
In another darkness you began
with familiar contours,
a specific fondness
for the sweet curve
of a jaw, the soft
inside of a thigh.
From these known shapes
your touch adjusts
to a shared darkness,
feeling out the intricate love
you have shaped
between yourselves.
But to these kicks
you extend a general love,
a love which requires
no other explanation.
Birth will complicate
this love, too, with details:
but for now it simply
is.

Entomology
Will's Poem

You came to a place where the woods, you said,
were pulsing with trees. Later, coming upon a pair
of grasshoppers immobilized in their stolid mating,

you told me that they were stacked like bunkbeds.
I sit for hours waiting on metaphor, like those
grasshoppers, paralyzed by the stubborn urge to create,

while you leap about in language, discovering
for the first time the pure ecstasy of words. This
is what I stopped to think. But you went to find a jar.

The grasshoppers looked so vulnerable, locked in their
secret knowledge, as if sex were an instinctive surrender
to death, but you thought only of the supreme pleasure

of bug-collecting, their pale-green bodies uncoupling
under glass. Like you, I often feel the urge to enclose
every natural act in some clear container, a poem,

something to remember by. You came of such an act,
such a longing to compose myself into something
separate and new, something I can no longer contain: you.

Cicadas

Slit down the back
like a plastic change purse
from which the cicada
has withdrawn its body's glisten,
the dry shape still clings
to tree bark, pompeiian,
surprised by self-eruption,
a mold into which one might pour
molten insect.
It rose in body like heat,
its high-tension drone
disembodied in the air:
song of buzz-saw and drill,
as if August were
a season under construction,
a scaffolding of dry skin
on the trees, the sky at dusk
a blueprint for fall.
Somewhere there has been
a resurrection,
but the only sign I have
is this calloused husk,
an abandoned house
whose inhabitant has gone
to attend the miracle.

Small World

Peter asked for clay.
All summer he built himself
little chairs, tables,
a drawbridge for his fort
in the backwoods, dreaming
of a bigger world
where he could build houses
big enough to live in,
big enough for everyone.
Happiness was a hammer
in his hand, saw and nails,
everything fitting together
snug and square. His
seven years had given him
strength and skill enough
to piece this much together.
He asked for clay,
and made himself
a model of the towers,
a place where he has never been.
He made them, he said,
for remembering:
things small enough to hold,
like the small white pawns
taken from a board, the toy-sized
city of ghosts left standing
at the foot of his bed
while he sleeps
and sometimes dreams
of picking up his hammer,
and of what he would build.

The Sacred Oaks

The Dakota had no documents, no bones
or artifacts filed among the roots, no map
to enclose the trees within a numbered grid
of sacred ground. It was the same old story:

oral tradition, stories told out like oak leaves
falling from disputed trees, becoming soil,
enriching nothing but this place on earth.

There was no telling the DOT that oaks
are sacred as lungs are sacred, their leaves
atoning in oxygen for the sin of highways,
or that their roots go back before treaties

into prairie earth, staking their own claim
against wind and fire, every ring around
the heartwood a notary's seal, a proof
of adaptation and survival. Now they are

gone, removed because they stood on a line
from A to B, the map's manifest destinations,
and in our haste to get there we could not
make a detour for the trees, or anything the earth

itself, without our human sanction, sanctifies.

River Bend

These places, like Old Testament miracles,
have ceased to exist, waiting for us
to recreate them. Like a prayer
the snow falls, my footsteps
scatter sparrows from the grass,
the ducks mumble over their pond. The prairie
cups itself to my ear, closes out the empty
stomach-rumble of the highway, and I hear
the grass voiced like an organ
with wind and birdsong, tongues of milkweed pod,
winter poised above me like a dark chord.

I come here with a heart in waiting,
to learn the patience of seeds sleeping
winterlong above the frozen earth, the patience
of Sarai waiting to be renamed into flower.
This prairie is a covenant renewed
in the earth, a promise delivered
in the voice of fire, just as Moses heard
the voice of God in the wilderness. Here
I listen to the requiem of snow, the earth
awaiting the resurrection of its dead,
the whisper of wings making angels in the air.

The Slaughter of the Innocents *1998*

These scenes from the life of Jesus
in crayon on the Sunday school walls
all lead to the same raw umber conclusion—
and red, if the children remember the nails
through his feet and hands. Once in a lifetime,
the minister says, you should try to imagine
the details of Christ's wounds—
the nail entering the palm, the shattered
tesserae of bone. But already twice this year
boys with guns have killed their classmates—
something we can't imagine. They were children
who could have colored the life of Jesus
in sixty-four brilliant colors—the turquoise blue
of the water he walked upon, the cerulean
of the heaven into which he rose. We can't
imagine what has taken those colors away
and left us with the plain black and white
of headlines, the blank spaces of our disbelief.

Girls' Night Out

No matter how much I scrub or cook,
housework is never alchemy enough
to grant me temporary change of flesh—
I'm always the admirable chimera,
never resolving into my grosser parts,
or never escaping them. The facts are
the facts. Our flesh genders us
for different conversations and sex
becomes untranslatable, nuanced as it is
by the experience of our bodies.
A conversation about bodies themselves
can mean different things in and out
of the idiom of desire.

               In short, I'm left alone
with the rhythm of the second hand
rubbing the clock toward midnight,
rounding to the nearest solitude,
nudging me closer and closer to myself.
Poor boy, with no story to tell of his first
period and likewise never knowing
with men how to begin a conversation
unless about a tool I need to borrow.
Could I get together with your husbands
and talk sensitively and with humor
about our first ejaculations?
It's not the same somehow, as if there were
poetry embodied in your moon rhythms
but not in the rough earthsongs we force
from ourselves.

Go sing yourselves back
into bodies and blood. I can only tune myself
to her body's hum, skirling out pleasure
like a round, becoming complete
with a voice sounding below and above.

Marjorie Rice

Her pentagons looked like houses
in the notation she devised—
a modest mathematical suburb
on California's tessellated coast.
In one house the stick figure of
a woman indicated the slide
and rotation of the angles,
as if she had inscribed herself
into her work, made herself
the symbol of a transformation:

because of the folding of sheets
and the setting of tables,
because of the daily reordering
of the same small pieces of her life,
because in dailiness she discovered
some idiomatic system of beauty,

her kitchen floor slowly puzzled itself
into a Moorish garden, as in Escher,
of hibiscus protracted into bloom.

*Marjorie Rice is a California homemaker who discovered fou previously unrecognized classes
of pentagons capable of tiling a plane.*

From the Animal Alphabet

No X for the Animal Alphabet,
Nothing between the

Whale and
Yak

Except the Xiphosuran,
Nearly fossilized in its
Intertidal landscape,

The last of its Order:
Limulus polyphemus,

The horseshoe crab,

Oddly obsolete
Silurian flotsam,
Its carapace

A relic of tides,
Elaborately evolved,
Perfected for eons

To arrive at this mute
Efficiency of survival.

But the children
Making their alphabets prefer
To imagine the

X-ray fish

And not

This stubborn,
Unglamorous,
Vestigial seaside
Wonder:
Xiphosuran.

Beethoven's Seventh *1978*

A pressed metallic iridescence
is not the same as the rainbow
etched in black vinyl, unravelling
to a smooth, repetitive silence.
A part of my life was mapped
in diamond dust, grooved latitudes
compassed with sound,
where I slid easily into belonging.
Now I long to return to that place
two and a half inches in
where the Allegretto begins
and the needle rides soft waves
of abraded sound, like the shuffle
of hands rubbed together for warmth.
That surface noise was my longing
tattooed into the music's whorled skin,
or my own fingerprint rubbing
against something eternal.

Ars Poetica While Waiting for the Appliance Repairman

These words will never fix anything.
Magic is only the wishful thinking of poets
who want to put their words to work—
to raise the dead, charm a lover,
animate their brooms to sweep the floor.

Amphion built the walls of Thebes
with a song that made the stones
haul themselves into a ring around him:
schist shifting out of faultlines,
blocks of granite wading out of fields,
self-quarried, metamorphic, clambering
onto each other's rough-hewn backs
to catch a glimpse of the poet, the builder—
held together by the mortar of his words.

These words will not even clear the dust
from the windowsill—they will simply point
it out, like a mother-in-law, like a rude guest.
They will insist upon it, like the sunlight
through this dirty window that sends it spinning.

What Comes Next
Poems 2002 - 2006

In a Japanese Room
Minneapolis Institute of Arts

I say, slow down and look.
I want him to see
how a painting creates focus,
distance, and a source of light,
how we are drawn
into a moment always
on the point of dissolution:
the knife poised above
the cake, the child ready
to blow out the candles,
the last instant before
the smoke and the crumbs
and the disappointment.
Look at the father, I say, his face
a blur of thick strokes,
an abstraction, a black suit
standing in the doorway.

How would I paint them,
these colorful groups
of first-graders swirling
through the galleries,
excited to find that beyond
every room is another
and another room, always
leading back to a place
where they have already been?
I know this will only happen
once, this moment,
perfect as it is,
when we find ourselves
in a Japanese room,

under the dark, carved beams,
where the furniture
stands in the foreground
of a paper screen
suggesting tranquil mountains
and light, voiceless birds—
an uninhabited space
where life is always an art,
so uncluttered of everything
but what we imagine it could be.

Outside, the city, the traffic,
the fifteen schoolbuses,
West Twenty-Fourth Street,
and not a single tranquil mountain.
I want to tell him, stay,
because I will fail you,
because I will never be perfect,
and God knows
what you will think of me.
But he hurries on, just happy
to be with his Dad
at the museum, looking
forward to a picnic in the park,
to the world of smoke and crumbs
and what comes next.

Lodestone

In eighth grade geoscience,
the boys and girls identify
minerals by their streak and lustre,
their hardness, heft and cleavage.
A girl holding a piece of magnetite
asks another girl, "When
was the first time it happened to you?"
and a boy at the same lab table asks,
"The first time what happened?"
The girls give him a dirty look,
and lean in close to whisper
whatever it is that both of them know.
A boy can't identify the streak
and heft of their conversation,
only that the mineral in her hand
is iron, magnetic, and possibly
the meteoric trace of life on Mars.
He knows it attracts. And girls,
he knows, are metamorphic:
or are they igneous, crystals
from some earthen fire, some deep
flow of magma, something
volcanic that gives them lustre,
cleavage, and a certain hardness?

Daywings

Ephemeroptera, (daywings)

In a net of late sunlight, mayflies
dip and rise, caught in the brief updraft
of mating, fizzling out
in a determined shimmer of wings.
What grace they have
is reserved for this hour before sunset,
the males casting themselves
into the current of air, the fly
fishing for another of its kind,
the females swung up under,
hooked into the dance of survival,
the air gilded with the light
of a thousand couplings. They swarm
like static amid disturbance of gulls,
morning dun still floating ashore
from their watery second birth,
their bodies winged for this one dance:
dying proof, if we need it, that beauty
is the upshot of our mortal business.
In the morning they'll be gone,
a million sparks burned down to ash,
littering the beach grass
with their flimsy one-night wings.

Index

Finally, I am indebted to my wife, Jane Anne,
for much help with all phases of the book,
especially with the preparation of the indexes.
—John T. Curtis, *The Vegetation of Wisconsin* (1959)

mornings, September,
New England asters
and stiff goldenrod
map the old fields with pollen,
conjuring prairie
from the sandy loam,
flares of sumac in the draws:

look up the flight
of the waxwing overhead,
seeding the grassland
with juniper,
spores of migration
taking root,
collating the prairie
and the pine forest
north to south,

and you will find
Jane Ann Curtis
with her index cards,
retracing
her husband's footsteps
page after page
into the undergrowth,
among ephemerals
dying back into shade,
and sometimes stumbling
on the poetry
of how the world

comes perfectly
together,

as in:

fern, sweet
ferns
fidelity

William Cullen Bryant

My heart is awed within me, when I think
Of the great miracle that still goes on.
                    Bryant, "Forest Hymn"

He was born to the cutting and clearing,
the old forests going down around him as he grew
into a love of the crepuscular and vanishing,
migrations, extinctions, the Indian and bison

diminishing west beyond the railhead,
the wilderness filling with the immigrant
drone of bees. We picture him in twilight,
gray as weathered clapboard, his face

an overgrown field in which the eyes
still burn a clearing, the patriarch
of old hymnals and abandoned farms,
the one-room schoolhouse and granite

death angels fallen among the weeds.
But clear away the dust and a forest
still covers half the continent, opening
onto prairie still unfurrowed by the plow,

and the pioneer who has gone further
than any white man before still imagines
that he is standing at the end of the world
or about to go back to the very beginning.

Diaspora

There was the time the precocious
watcher of Bill Nye the Science Guy
tried to build a Duplo helix that kept
falling apart until frustration made him
pitch the blocks in rage across the room,
expelling them from his childhood's Eden.
Those Duplo sent their scatterlings
to colonize the underdust of furniture,
the dry squalls of the ductwork,
into the four corners of every room
like the sons of Noah from the wreckage
of some unbuildable ark. Sometimes,
now that the children are grown
much closer to their own scattering,
I still stumble upon the singular Robinson Duplo,
colorful old-timer with his beard of dust,
the last survivor of a time when we believed
we could still make everything fit.

Aeneas

to my Father
Robert B. Hardy, Jr. (1930-2005)

I went downtown last night with Mother and Ellen. We got you a
pair of gray pants at Edwards. They are a gray check. You may
think they look a bit loud when you first see them, but remember
that clothes don't look as loud when worn as when off. They are
a fine pair of pants and I'm sure you will like them. We also got
you a literal translation of the Aeneid. Let us know how it helps
out.

—Letter from my grandfather to my father
at Cornell University, October 19, 1948

You were never loud, only worn and gray,
something passed along to us at birth, incidental
article of parentage—or so we always thought
when we saw you translated into a dead language
in our midst. Your epic was a series of small
upstate towns—Ulysses, Hector—allusions
in the landscape to some heroic faithfulness,
some checkered fabric of loss and hopefulness,
something not always appreciated at first sight.

How often the miles bled from your heart,
the highway your martyrdom, the landscape
indifferent behind its scrim of rain, kept awake
by the self-flagellation of the windshield wipers.
You came home to an absence that grew
until your return no longer filled it.

Exhaustion rubbed the nap from your easy chair,
wore away all the surfaces where we touched—
we watched you erode. If you were Odysseus,
where were your stories? There was no Circe,

no suitors, no Sirens: only the radio turned up
loud enough to keep you awake behind the wheel.

There was no war. We never went out to find you.

We never understood your sacrifice, always
exchanging love for duty, that estrangement
which we could never see as the price of your
devotion. If we seem to turn away, it is only
because you have given us this road, far-flung
sparks of smoldering Troy's self-consuming fire.

Learning Curve

All my high school teachers have retired
to the golf course now. My science teacher
tends the clubhouse bar, still standing
as I remember him, behind a laboratory table,
mixing. If you ask, he can still explain,
on the back of a cocktail napkin, precisely
how the ball must precisely curve to reach the cup:
there are no straight lines, my art teacher
could tell you, in golf or in working with clay—
only the curve of your body over the wheel,
the curve of your hands, the arc of your swing,
the pot, the ball's trajectory, the earth.
My science teacher could explain about gravity,
which the ball never escapes, always falling
in accordance with laws which the golfer
feels in his swing, in the weight of his club,
in the movement of air, as the potter knows
the pot from the feel of the clay in her hands,
the movement of the wheel, the completed arc,
the hole into which it falls. In twenty years
I have almost caught up to where I left them,
on the cusp of middle age, so far from where
I thought I'd fall: there are no straight lines,
only the arc of our lives constantly changing.

Postcard to Crawford, Texas, from the Les Cheneaux Islands, Michigan

Surrounded by water,
we don't think much about the desert
or how to make one.

The sunsets and the stars
humble us with their presence—
because we know these are God's banners,
and not the flags we raise with our own hands.

We live with the bats
and the spiders, and cannot hate
what is so much a part of the place
and our own history.

We don't do much clearing,
because sometimes the world works
by letting things grow

and with a simple love of where we are:

surrounded by Huron's waters,
the cedar forest, and each other.

Wish you were here.

The Acts of the Apostles

"Ladies and gentlemen, circumcised and uncircumcised…"
Peter warmed up the crowd with tongues of flame, told jokes,
performed a few small miracles—though the hecklers in the crowd
kept demanding resurrections. Backstage, Paul was getting loose,
juggling his rubber balls—first three, then four, then five at once
(one ball was Faith and another, Love): and if he dropped a ball,
it bounced, and he knew how to make it seem intentional.
Harder still were the knives: he had to make it appear graceful,
the steel blades flashing, the fine-honed edge of redemption.
But nothing in his act was harder than juggling the spirit and the
                                                        law—
he couldn't do it like Jesus did, making everything seem
equally light. A scattering of applause, and Peter stepped off stage
wiping the sweat from his brow. "It's a tough crowd," he said,
as Stephen stepped out to deliver his dramatic monologue.
It wasn't long before the boos and the beer bottles thrown on stage.
Paul was trying to remember the one about the two Corinthians
who walk into a bar—and what was the one Jesus always told
about love? It was so simple, but he was famous for that.
He had that knack for holding an audience in the palm of his hand.

Oh, Brave New World
for Peytie McCandless

she laughs at the world, or applauds, or boos—
she's the first to stand for the ovation, and the first
to throw rotten vegetables onto the stage—

she stops each prejudice, each injustice, asking
it to move a little to the left
to make room for the entrance of wonder—

or she's up in the catwalk, tossing out fistfuls
of soap powder snow
that fall through the blue lights of winter—

and in the second act, when the seasons change,
and the last stray flake comes drifting down,
unseasonable among the budding trees,

we watch in wonder as her heart changes everything,
and the accidental snowflake
becomes the first white blossom blown

from the boughs of spring, and the grass grows
green beneath her feet, and the walls fall away,
and we believe her when she says the world is new.

Fudgesicle

In memory of my father

He can still make his scissors say "bread,"
paring away the word
from its picture in the weekly specials,
cutting holes to represent his hunger
for the thing itself, now that he's lost
his taste for naming.
He fills an envelope with pictures
to represent fulfillment—

a full loaf,
a gallon of milk—

and my mother does his shopping,
coming back as always with her arms full
of unspoken things.

He's lost weight, too—
as if the fat were in the words
he no longer uses, as if the extra pounds
were simply forgotten—
like the word for fudgesicle.

I remember him saying once, angry
when my siblings and I had eaten all the fudgesicles
without leaving the last one for him:
"You know how I love fudgesicles!"

I don't remember him
ever saying how much he loved me.
But now that he's lost the word
for "fudgesicle," I realize that what he really loves
was long ago
already beyond words.

The Life That Is
Poems 2007-2011

To the Daughter I Never Had

I saw you today at the playground.
You were wearing a little dress
that reminded me of all the dresses

I never bought for you,
all the sundresses and twirly skirts,
all the Hanna Anderson.

You were on the swing, leaning back,
reaching up with your candy-striped legs,
as if to reinsert yourself

into an imaginary heaven,
into the realm of possibility.
You didn't see me watching you

from a future in which you don't exist,
but sometimes you smile at me
from the face of another man's daughter—

a smile that contains all the mornings
we never baked bread together,
all the cartwheels you never turned,

all the stories you never told me
about all the things that never happened.
You are six, or nine, or fifteen, and always

as beautiful as I imagined, growing up
smart and graceful and strong, and I am glad,
and it breaks my heart

that you have become all this without me.

I have spent what would have been
your entire life breaking up

fights between the boys,
scrubbing the floor around the toilet,
trying to get them to change their underwear,

and knowing that I could not love anyone more—
not even you.
Perhaps someday you will understand

how it's possible to regret
the life that never was, and still love nothing
more than the life that is.

Midlife Crisis While Watching a Nature Program (*Octopus marginatus*)

On the one hand, look at all you've accomplished:
career, house, children, money in the bank.
Your life has taken a certain comfortable shape
and there isn't all that much you'd wish to change.
On the other hand, you will never be a marine biologist,
scanning the ocean floor with your submersible camera,
on the lookout for an octopus walking on two legs.
Your eyes will never widen behind your mask,
and you will never gesture in slow-motion
to your fellow marine biologist, the water champagning
with the excitement of your quickened breath,
because you have just seen what looks like a coconut
sauntering along the ocean floor with a purposeful stride
that makes you think of John Cleese with tentacles
and a coconut suit. No predator with a taste for sushi
will go after a coconut rolling along with the current,
water-logged terrestrial junk, not worth a second glance.
But your human heart goes out to the octopus:
no bones, no spine, nothing but head and feet,
and a brain devoted entirely to escaping notice—
little sea-nerd on rubbery legs, pretending to be tough.
You admire something so soft and determined,
so adaptable. How wonderful not to mind
how ridiculous you look, to be self-contained
like an octopus. How much harder for humans
to adapt. Especially now, when we are who we are,
when we will never be marine biologists looking
in astonishment at the octopus disguised as a coconut—
when we can only look out the window at the boat
our middle-aged neighbor suddenly brought home
when his wife had left him and his children had all grown up.

Asanas

Out by the highway substation, road salt on the wires
completed the circuit, and the wooden pole burst into flames.
Lights went out all over town. At the yoga studio,
we moved through *asanas* by candlelight—
the Pigeon, the Child, the Downward Facing Dog—
but I, with tight hamstrings and herniated disk,
could only manage the Burning Utility Pole:
the high tension, pain exploding down my spine.

A Typical Poem

A typical poem
thinks about sex
every six lines.

Don't be fooled
by its apparent
preoccupation

with blackbirds
or wheelbarrows—
it's really about sex.

It watches the autumn
trees undressing,
winter's white body—

and spring, which,
with its birdsong and blooming,
is all about sex. The wildflowers,

the lilacs, the linden blossoms in June—
spring is a multiple orgasm, and the typical
poem can think of nothing else amidst all the

pornography of nature. Sex becomes its only theme:
the buds unfastening like bras, the flowering and deflowering,
the spent magnolia blossoms dropped like used condoms in the grass.

Jane Austen's Toes

"There is, for instance, no mention of toes in any of her work...
Nor are there any hips, thighs, shins, buttocks, kidneys, intestines,
wombs, or navels..."
—Carol Shields, *Jane Austen* (2001)

Jane Austen never mentions toes,
although she must sometimes
have thought about her own—
blistered, perhaps, and sore
from walking in pattens with wooden soles,
especially (one would guess)
under the ball of her big toe,
just where the arch of the foot begins—
though such details are absent from her books.

I'm not surprised she never mentions
intestines or kidneys. I myself prefer
to let them do their work
unimagined. And somehow
the absence of a womb
in her work is unsurprising.
We are left to imagine, if we must,
Mr. Darcy discovering Elizabeth's toes,
along with her hips and thighs,
her nipples and navel,
and all the other parts
the author never mentions—
the body beginning where the novel ends.

We can infer from letters
that she herself possessed a body—
she mentions stockings, shoes,
shawls, shifts, and stays
("not made to force the bosom up at all"),
the soft sibilant shuffle of silks—

though even clothing
can become tiresome.
"I hate describing such things,"
she says of a bonnet.

Her women are embodied
mostly in words, in the delicacy
and daring of language. Even Fanny,
for most of the novel nothing
but silence and scruples,
begins to materialize—
not when men start to notice her looks,
but when she finds her voice.

It's the voice we think of,
not the body or even the face
in Cassandra's watercolor
that we want to think of as pretty.
Standing at the foot
of her grave, we find it hard
to imagine a body
lies there at all. The stone
mentions only her soul,
her character, and her intellect,
but is silent on the subject of her bones.

Mark Twain and Dorothy Quick Sit for Photographs *1907*

It was beautiful, surpassingly beautiful, enchantingly beautiful;
and now it is lost, and I shall not see it any more.
It is a matter of sex, I think.
Mark Twain, *Eve's Diary 1906*

In the beginning of another century,
they sat in the garden, her head on his shoulder,
her white dress drifting against his white suit,
snowflake and glacier, two clean white pages,
as if he were God, and she an outgrowth of His own rib,

Adamless. She was the first of the well-behaved
little girls he collected in old age—his Angelfish,
floating decorously in white dresses through
his billiard room, or sitting for photographs, their bodies
a concentration of chemicals and sunlight. Here,

he holds a cigar in his right hand, and she holds a black
box in her lap—a purse or a Brownie camera—
and it is hard with our post-Freudian eyes not to read
sex into the picture, lurking symbolically like a snake.
Puberty would expel them from his garden. His angels

would fall into bodies that marked time, and would only
remind him he was old. He wanted them to stay
as they were in photographs, shimmering beside him,
white on white, a comet for the beginning
and the end of life. He collected them in the photographer's

black box, the bright images of his Angelfish swimming
out of darkness, their white bodies developing
into pure absence. Here, his cigar will never burn down,
and can never be enjoyed, and the photograph can only show
                                                        him his desire

to possess an innocence he has already lost.

Old Memorial Field

The old football field is silvered
with dandelions gone to seed.
In this light, it looks like ice inside

the oval of the overgrown track—
seeds scatter and skate, silk skirts
spinning above slippered toes, swirling

and melting on a sudden breeze.
The wind in the cottonwood
sounds like running water,

or the echo of October applause
as the ghostly seeds break their huddle
and drift into the end zone—

dispersing like a crowd at the end
of the game, or like graduates, leaving
behind their empty chairs—

caps and tassels flung in the air,
a million plans suspended in celebration,
coming down to take root somewhere else.

Climate Change

How few poems I've written during the Bush years!
I've sat out the mild winters in silence,
distrustful of the early springs, the shock and awe
of summer days invading March.
I suppose I should have said something sooner,
but I would have felt like such a grump
complaining about the January shirt-sleeve weather—
like the gloom-eyed groundhog making
his discredited case for six more weeks of winter.
That's the problem with liberals like me—
we live in cold states, under gray flaking clouds,
and so we start to think in shades of gray.
Maybe we should lighten up, enjoy the early spring.
I was never planning to visit a glacier anyway.
Then why do I miss so much those light
April snows of the Clinton years, white on green
like a Wellstone lawn sign, the waffling season
of winter in the morning, spring in the afternoon?

School Day Blues

For years, my writing desk faced west.
In the morning, I watched the Episcopal Church
lay the shadow of its cross on the parking lot across the street,
double-parked among the all-night permit holders.
As the sun rose it withdrew its blessing
to the middle of the street, crossing the traffic,
a smudge of ash thumbing penitential hoods.
The steeple at noon stood shadowless like the needle
of a gauge, showing the day half-empty.
In those first days of school, I often pushed
my shadow down the sidewalk like an empty stroller,
or spent long hours watching the cross's shadow
wade against the current of the sun, waiting
to receive my own belated blessing. But now
my desk faces east, and in the morning I watch
other children waiting at the corner for the bus to come
like a clumsy vanishing act, leaving nothing but
a wisp of exhaust and a mother who looks both ways
before she walks her own long shadow across the street.

Bluestem

Every year, the grass.
In the fall,
so bronze,
lifting the light back to the sun.
In the spring,
greening out of the burn,
out of the blackest earth.
From April to September
grown so tall
I could lose myself in it.
All flesh is grass,
and its beauty
like the flower of the field.
But can I burn like this
every time
and come back golden?
I want to walk out
into the prairie,
beyond flesh,
beyond wanting,
so far that I forget
what it was
that brought me there—
the burning,
even the need to forget.
Nothing but the black earth
and the light lifted back to itself.

Fifty

In celebration of the 50ᵗʰ Anniversary of the Northfield Arts Guild

Unless, like Nicolas Copernicus,
it happens to be your birthday,
no one celebrates February 19th,
the fiftieth day of the year.
Fifty is ordinary, not golden
(the atomic number of tin)
and not even as old as it once was:
fifty, we are told, is the new thirty.
Sure, fifty has some interesting
mathematical properties—
it's the smallest sum
of two squares in two different ways—
but fifty percent is still only half:
half-hearted, half-empty,
a failing grade on any scale.
So I suppose what we celebrate,
after all, is not completion,
but the brief moment of equipoise
and everything that falls on either side—
so much putting up and taking down;
so many rehearsals,
the striking of so many sets;
so many lumps of clay,
so many empty bowls to fill.
What matters most in this poem
may be the word "unless,"
or it may be the shape of the whole—
the performance, the painting in its frame,
the bowl that you fill
with whatever part of yourself
you offer to the experience of art.
Or the most important part
may be what happens next,

when the poem supposedly ends,
and there is still so much more to say.

Catullus 2

Passer, deliciae meae puellae,
quicum ludere, quem in sinu tenere,
cui primum digitum dare appetenti
et acris solet incitare morsus,
cum desiderio meo nitenti
carum nescio quid lubet iocari
et solaciolum sui doloris,
credo ut tum gravis acquiescat ardor:
tecum ludere sicut ipsa possem
et tristis animi levare curas!

Sparrow, my sweetheart's sweetheart,
her plaything, perched in her lap,
poised to give a sharp peck
to the fingertip she raises:
it pleases her, my lustrous girl,
to play this game of endearments.
It keeps her mind off her sorrows,
and I think it makes the sting of love a little less.
If only I could play with you as she does,
and lift this load of sadness from my heart.

Nest

I keep thinking today
will be different:
the poem I write
will have long lines
and won't refer to itself.
It will reach out its long arms
to embrace the world.
My poem won't be about birds,
but the birds themselves
will carry my poem,
line by line,
to build their nests.
The oriole will lay her eggs
in my poem—
ink-scribbled,
parchment-colored eggs,
like the fragments
of some medieval manuscript.
But there will be no similes
in my poem, —
only the oriole herself
and her fragile eggs.

Ballast
Poems 2012-2016

Worm

"All of the terrestrial earthworms in Minnesota
are non-native, invasive species."
 —*Minnesota Department of Natural Resources*

I sent my friend an article about earthworms.

She said she would rather
read about earthworms than think
about the man who left her,
the father of her children.

She said it gave her a different perspective
on earthworms to learn that they consume
the rich organic duff, the slow

accumulation of years that makes
the soil hospitable to life.

He left her for a woman half his age,
a girl just out of high school,
not much older than his own daughter.

She found it interesting how the worms first arrived
in soil from Europe used to ballast ships—
the ships taking on cargo in the New World,
the worm-infested soil dumped out on the shore.

It makes you question everything you thought was true.

You counted on something to be good,
to make life richer with time—
but last weekend she changed all the locks.

It makes you wonder about the ballast you carry.

The Former State Demographer Presents Ten-Year Enrollment Projections for the Northfield Public Schools

The old demographer,
projecting cohort survivals far
beyond her own life's natural span,
looks into a future without her,
knowing that one of those columns
of data contains her own death.
She knows her days are numbered.
But there is no room for sentimentality
in the old demographer's numbers,
no mourning or celebration,
only whatever professional optimism
there is in assuming the world
will still be here for the projected .
graduating class of 2025.
She knows there will come a time
when the children and grandchildren
will rent a dumpster, sell the books,
walk one last time through rooms
as empty as the cells of a blank
spreadsheet that some other family
will fill with resident live births:
a new cohort hovering off
to kindergarten, graduating,
moving into single-family houses,
having children, sinking down
through the slow column of years
to their own statistical graves.

September—

Sept—the sound of summer
striking its last match to burn
a few more bright days down
to the *ember* of October trees.

Zoom

for my niece Annina

On Google Maps,
East Amherst, New York,
is circled in clouds.
I think of you
under one of those clouds,
looking up at the gray underside,
the puffy white,
the silver lining—
or thinking that this one
looks like an elephant,
outracing its shapeless herd
across the sky's blue savannah.
I think of you wondering
whether these clouds
mean clearing skies,
or more rain coming.
From above, the clouds
look like cartoon sheep,
grazing the suburban grid,
like the empty bubbles
of comic strip thoughts.
I zoom in closer,
and the clouds dissolve,
like a cloud of breath
on a winter morning.
I see rooftops arranged
like a shell game
on green cul-de-sacs.
Closer still, I see Mighty Taco,
Sapphire Salon,
All Natural Chiropractic and
Spinal Decompression—
but I still can't find you.

Rarely have we come together
into the awkwardness
of family gatherings,
slipping into the strange
almost-selves we reserve
for such fraught occasions.
Most of your life
has happened at a distance,
someone else's weather.
So I think of you now
among the clouds, floating
above the noose of streets,
the dull gravity of days,
your dreams forming
into words and actions
that will make some
parched landscape flower.

Georgic

Last night, unable to sleep, I read
Virgil's instructions for care of the soil:
how to rotate crops of legumes and grain,
how to burn off stubble from the land—

but every time I closed my eyes, my brain
composed another email, managed to spoil
sleep with some unfinished business, and
obsessed over things I never should have said.

So many worries, so much turmoil,
so many thoughts that buzzed inside my head:
I tried to picture Mantua, the land
resplendent with the lupines and the grain,

the curved scythe swinging in the reaper's hand,
the fire burning off the dry stalks that remain—
and, finally, the farmer trudging off to bed,
and sleep that brings relief from all his daily toil.

Agnostic Psalm

Agnosticism
is a harder discipline
than faith.
Watching the maple wings spin
free of their parent shade,
I can imagine God more easily
than the laws of science.
Sir Isaac himself—
scientific method
be damned! —
may have seen this seed
as a key, turning
in the clockmaker's hand,
winding the invisible
springs of gravity.
Even physics has
its fallen angels,
its hard facts
lapsing into metaphor.

I know I am no
more than what I am:
a monkey once-removed,
an iteration of primordial dust.
I know this,
and still find comfort
in songs of exile,
these seeds
hanging from the maples
like unstrung lyres.

Good Friday Walk

Walking along the path,
through the old field overgrown
with pigeon grass and dry

stalks of sceptered goldenrod,
with each step I raised
an eruption of flickers from the grass,

a flash of yellow underwing,
white rump hoisting its flag of retreat.
I thought each one of them

had to be the last, but still another
and another launched itself
into the arms of the leafless trees.

Finally, I stopped,
with dozens of flickers still
rising from the brown earth all around.

I stood with my arms outstretched,
as if I had opened myself, and released
all these startled, earth-colored birds.

The Tomb Scene

I was a boy
who picked flowers —
peonies, lilacs, wild roses—
beauty I arranged
for myself in secret,
like most adolescent
arrangements.
I learned that loneliness
was a kind of beauty—
loneliness of moon,
loneliness of summer,
loneliness of rain
on a Saturday afternoon,
listening to the Met,
Rhadames and Aïda
buried alive,
their last breaths
squandered on song.

The Fall of Troy

Parodos from *Oresteia*
adapted from Aeschylus

Scattered across the plain of Troy,
the fires were like stars burning out—
each fire a body burning,
each one a world coming to an end.
Smoke spread like night across the plain,
blackened the city walls and rose,
like the dark spectre of an army
raising its siege engines to the walls:
as smoke the Greeks first entered Troy.
Now each ship that sails from Troy
brings home its cargo of ashes.
The men who left home in bright helmets
and breastplates of shining bronze
come home again in little pots of clay.

For ten years
the women have waited,
husbanding their fields and farms,
counting their losses,
looking up from their work
to see black sails on the horizon.
A generation has fallen at Troy,
another generation in Greece has grown up fatherless.
Little boys have grown up thinking absence
is what it means to be a man.
Little girls have grown up learning
the name of Helen like a curse.
The birds that descend on the new-sown fields
are Helen's fault; the month without rain,
the hen that stops laying,
the wind that blows dust in the door—
Helen is the name of every misfortune.

The flames that dance
destruction through the streets of Troy
first burned in the mind of Zeus
when Paris came
and carried Helen from her husband's bed.
The anger of Zeus followed him home like a lighted fuse.

And after Helen went the Greeks:
walled cities emptied of their men,
forests stripped to build the fleet,
cattle butchered, fields laid bare,
treasuries plundered of their bronze—
the wealth of Greece sent as a dowry of war.
Now every home that sent a man to Troy
has its urn, a handful of ashes paid
for what was once a husband, or a son.

Performed by The Carleton Players at Carleton College,
Northfield, Minnesota, May 2012; and by Hero Now Theatre,
Minneapolis, Minnesota, September 2016.

The Old Field

No more cows to keep down weeds
and keep the acorn from becoming oak,
no more tractor, no more plow that broke
the plain, just birds dispersing seeds
beyond the fence post's broken line,
the bursting milkweed pod, the breeze,
the burs on socks, the pollinating bees,
the squirrels, the buried nuts, and time.
All the effort, all the farmer's labor to defend
his land against the fast encroaching wild—
there's goldenrod where once he tilled:
the work of human hands undone by wind.

Bloodroot

Waiting for the bloodroot to rise
and constellate in April woods,
leaves pushing up through leaf mold
into uncertain warmth,
like small hands raised in supplication to the sun—

but the bloodroot asks for nothing,
only rises, earth's warmth nudging it toward light.

Willow

There was a weeping willow.
Curtained in green, as if we had found ourselves
a private room in the middle of the square,
we kissed and drank champagne
while the square emptied and the white
folding chairs from commencement
stood like cenotaphs to mark so many departures.
We were the last people left, abandoned by the rapture
of late spring in a college town,
the bubbles of champagne not quite enough to carry us away.

Thirty years have passed since then,
half as many since your brother called
to say he found my letters in the things you left behind
and it seemed we might have once been close.
We came close to so many things.
Returning after thirty years, married half my life,
with a son the age that we were then,
I looked for that willow, thinking how it must have grown
grand and almost Shakespearean in its attitude of grief.
But it was gone. The square was a false memory—
the chairs in a different place, and different people.
So this is what it's like: the world without us.

Consider

Consider how we fold
the fitted sheet.
It takes the two of us,
starting with so much
space between us,
holding the corners,
bringing them together,
hands meeting in the middle.

To the Black Boy at Summer Camp *1977*

In memory of Philando Castile

I was the only white kid
at the camp that summer—
a day camper who arrived in the morning
and went home in the afternoon.
All the other kids were bussed
from the city for a week of woods
and water and clean Upstate air.
My mother thought it would be good for me.
I was twelve years old and never
knew a black kid before
you told me we were enemies.
You never left my side all day,
telling me how much I hated you.
The next day I refused to go back.
I was too afraid.
What if I had gone back the next day
and the next, accepting this
as what I had to do?
Would I have begun to understand
what you were telling me?
I don't even remember your name—
but this morning when I learned the name
of another black man killed,
I wanted to go back and say to you:
I'm ready to listen.
We've only just met,
but there's history between us.

Baptisia alba

I walked out to the prairie
past bur oaks singing with orioles
and stood looking across acres
of white false indigo
at the solstice moon rising.
A congregation of white flowers,
immersed in prairie grass and moonlight.
It's been ten years since I stopped going to church
and these are still my metaphors.
I opened my hands again to let go of God,
and a lightning bug landed on my open palm.

The Acting Cashier

One hundred forty years ago, he was deposited in this ground
like a bond that bears its interest once a year.
As if a time-lock had opened, the street in front of the bank
fills with the citizens of 1876. At scheduled times,
unreconstructed outlaws spur their horses into town,
shots are fired, and Joseph Lee Heywood lives
his last moments for the crowd. At night, carnival lights
illuminate the town. But before the crowds have gathered,
here in this quieter place, we remember an ordinary man—
a man who worked and prayed with other ordinary people,
who in his ordinariness might never have been known
if a single moment hadn't cast him as a hero. We cannot all
be heroes, but we can all be so remarkably ordinary—
so humble, so generous in giving of ourselves, so steadfast
in our refusal to stand aside for what we know is wrong.
Who was this man who lies in the vaulted earth beneath our feet?
We can only know him by knowing each other.
The faithfulness of his life cannot be reenacted,
it can only be lived. This is the dividend he pays:
his life, divided among all of us, to be lived together.

Read at the grave of Joseph Lee Heywood on September 7, 2016,
the 140th anniversary of his death defending the First National
Bank (Northfield, Minnesota) against the James-Younger Gang.

Building Blocks

"Establishing a lasting peace is the work of education."
—*Maria Montessori*

Last night I woke to thunder.
Safe under my roof, I lay awake
listening as it rolled eastward,
followed by the peacefulness of rain.
In the morning, children bloomed
in bright colors on the bus corners,
teachers in still classrooms waited
for the calm to shatter into life.
There in the bustle and the noise
were the beginnings of peace.
Elsewhere, bombs fall and scatter
fear, like shrapnel edging
closer to our hearts. If all we carry
from the rubble is our hate,
then this is what we build. We close
the borders of ourselves. But last night
I heard a young Assyrian woman,
whose father's village had been bombed,
whose people had suffered
from centuries of genocide and war,
talk about Montessori school,
where she learned that we
must be the building blocks of peace.
Montessori had such a simple idea:
teach our children to make peace,
and let them show us how it's done.

The Shepherds

On Christmas Eve,
we sat in our bathrobes
on the closet floor,
pretending to be the shepherds
watching our flocks by night.
Above us, our clothes
were a multitude
of the heavenly host,
hovering on bent wire wings.
We still believed in those angels
and in the good news
that somewhere
a child was born.
The world was still small enough
to contain such miracles,
and expectation
could still sanctify this ordinary night.
We crouched there
on the closet floor,
as sometimes
in school we crouched
beneath our desks, imagining
something other than angels
coming down from the sky.
In the fetal position, we acted out
our beginning and our end.
But every year, at the darkest time,
the angels told us not to be afraid.
And when we took them down
from the rack of heaven
and put them on,
those angels were ourselves.

Acknowledgements

Grateful acknowledgement is made to the editors of the journals and anthologies in which the following poems originally appeared:

"Naturalization," *100 Words.*
"Packing the Creche," "Cicadas and The Slaughter of the Innocents," ©1998 and 1999, *The Christian Century*
"Domestication," *Minnesota Monthly*
"Falling," *To Love One Another*, ed. Ginny Lowe Connors (Grayson Books 2002); *Proposing on the Brooklyn Bridge*, ed. Ginny Lowe Connors (Grayson Books 2003).
"Essential Love," *Essential Love*, ed. Ginny Lowe Connors (Grayson Books 2000)
"Entomology," "River Bend," "The Sacred Oaks," "Girls' Night Out," and "Majorie Rice," *33 Minnesota Poets*, ed. Monica and Emilio DeGrazia (Nodin Press 2000)
"Small World," *Black Bear Review*
"Beethoven's Seventh, 1978," *North Coast Review*
"In a Japanese Room" and "Lodestone," in *The English Journal*, © 2002 and 2004, The National Council of Teachers of English
"Daywings" and "William Cullen Bryant," *Interdisciplinary Studies in Literature and the Environment (ISLE)*
"Index" and "Aeneas," *The Comstock Review*
"Learning Curve," *The Teacher's Voice*
"Postcard to Crawford, Texas, from the Les Cheneaux Islands, Michigan," *Water-Stone Review*
"The Acts of the Apostles," *Green Blade*
"Fudgesicle," *Beyond Forgetting: Poetry and Prose About Alzheimer's Disease*, ed. Holly Hughes (Kent State University Press, 2009)
"To the Daughter I Never Had," *Rattle*
"Midlife Crisis While Watching a Nature Program," *Red Cedar Review*
"A Typcial Poem," *Red Cedar*

"Jane Austen's Toes" and Mark Twain and Dorothy Quick Sit for Photographs, 1907" *Apple Valley Review*
"Bluestem," *Thirty-Two*
"Nest," *West Branch*
"Worm" and "Georgic," *IthacaLit*
"The Former State Demographer Presents Ten-year Enrollment Projections for the Northfield Public Schools" and "Good Friday Walk," in *Poetic Strokes*
"September" and "Consider," Northfield Sidewalk Poetry Project
"Agnostic Psalm," *The Whirlwind Review*
"The Fall of Troy" appears in *Aeschylus, The Oresteia: An Adaptation by Rob Hardy* (Hero Now Theatre, 2017).

Several poems also appeared in my chapbook, *The Collecting Jar* (Grayson Books 2005), the winner of the 2005 Grayson Books Poetry Chapbook Competition.

www.ingramcontent.com/pod-product-compliance
Lightning Source LLC
Chambersburg PA
CBHW022026090426
42739CB00006BA/306